T0102839

NOW THAT DREAMS
ARE BORN

NOW THAT DREAMS ARE BORN

Ify Omalicha

Order this book online at www.trafford.com
or email orders@trafford.com

Most Trafford titles are also available at major online book retailers.

© Copyright 2009 Ify Omalicha.
All rights reserved. No part of this publication may be reproduced, stored in a retrieval system, or
transmitted, in any form or by any means, electronic, mechanical, photocopying, recording, or
otherwise, without the written prior permission of the author.

Note for Librarians: A cataloguing record for this book is available from Library
and Archives Canada at www.collectionscanada.ca/amicus/index-e.html

Printed in Victoria, BC, Canada.

ISBN: 978-1-4251-8872-6

*Our mission is to efficiently provide the world's finest, most comprehensive book publishing
service, enabling every author to experience success. To find out how to publish your book, your
way, and have it available worldwide, visit us online at www.trafford.com*

Trafford rev. 10/29/2009

www.trafford.com

North America & international
toll-free: 1 888 232 4444 (USA & Canada)
phone: 250 383 6864 ♦ fax: 812 355 4082

NOW THAT DREAMS ARE BORN

*To God
Whose kingdom
Belongs to the children.*

Omalicha

Foreword

It gives me immense pleasure to be asked to write a Foreword to the third collection of poems by one of the most forward-looking of the present generation of young leaders, Ify Omalicha, a distinguished product of the University of Ibadan, where I taught for a few decades.

Ify, in this collection, has displayed her mastery of the poetic craft, but, in addition to this, she has shown a commitment to equity, fairplay and justice which is manifest in her very sensitive treatment of children and children's lives. In this regard the title poem and a number of others are exceptional.

All the poems have a freshness which keeps the readers on the alert from the beginning to the end of the collection, and there is a touch of a philosophical commitment to a future that will be more just and more noble and less riddled with the problems of premature soldiering and premature deaths due to the carelessness and recklessness of the older generation.

The poet, above all, brings to us the scintillating beauty of Nature and of a reproved Mankind. Both in the few long poems and in the many short ones, the poet helps us, as readers, to identify with her aspiration for a world that would be less riddled with oppresion and disasters. She gives due praise to bodies like **Save the Children, International Red Cross & Crescent, UNICEF,** and other organisations, that are committed to making the world a better and safer place to live in in the future.

Ify has, in this collection, proven the triumph of

optimism in a world beridden by unexpected disasters and wanton violence. She has asserted that God's Kindom belongs to the children. This is not only a prayer: it is the belief of all of us who identify with the motto of making the world a better place.

Ify Omalicha's new collection, *Now that Dreams are Born*, has my unreserved commendation. The combination of sensuousness and tactile beauty is startling and sincere. She is a poet who has a fund of affection for children and whose work will continue to thrill and challenge us all.

DAPO ADELUGBA
Department of Theatre and Performing Arts,
Ahmadu Bello University, Zaria,
Kaduna State, Nigeria

Author's Note

  The children are speaking with the look in their eyes but we're rushing past, chasing after treasures we may never own. It is time we slowed down for we must listen. Until then...

Chi aboọla
Let the snoring morn
Wake up to the cry of the child.

Omalicha

You have come

i

When the night squints in slumber
When the night's snooze lingers longer
Men dig for new life in the loins of maidens

When the dew falls on the eye-lids of morning
When morning yawns aloud
Maiden seek birth on their sacred mats

The walls are silent
Not asking who would come tend them
When age begins to wrinkle their skin
The walls are deaf to the groans of passion
Calling for escape

Men and maidens ruffle their mats
Their veins pant in their bones
Bones quake in their marrow
Blood boils hot in its pipe
Bound in ecstasy
They touch the heart of bliss

Waiting on the brim of hope

Praying

With hands stretched to the heavens
Pleading

Omalicha

If only *Chukwu okike*
Would empty his jars of clay. . .

Then sweat mingles with tears and blood
And ties
With a medley of sweet pain
       and deep moaning
Hearts throbbing
in a thousand rhythms of laughter. . .

The child has come.

Omalicha

ii

Hear me calling
Neighbour

run to me with dancing feet
  with your waist adorned
    in exotic wrapper and coral beads

run to me neighbour
  like a warrior honours the call
    of a sonorous drum

Bring with you clapping palms
  And a calabash
    of *uli* and white chalk

Swift on your heels
Neighbour mine

Let the charcoal burn the pot black
  Let the pot float in the stream
    Leave the wares lost in the market place
      Let the wood lay in the forest

The cry of my child
has SHATTERED the walls of shame
    draping me in robes of pride

Swift on your heels
 Neighbour mine

The sweet cry of my child
      calls you to a feast.

Omalicha

iii

Seeing that the fingers
are not even in their length

You chose to come

Knowing that the seasons
of rain and harmattan
bring changing tide

You chose to come

Against the threat of the wind
raising dust in the pathway
Against the howling of the storm
spitting bubbles in your face

You chose to come

Against the prickling thorns
lurking in vanishing treasures

You chose to come

Nwa m nnọ
for you have walked well
through the high and low plains
to begin your own journey

And on this seventh day of life
I call you
Oyín dà m'óla
Omo ni wúrà

                                                    Omalicha

káàbò.
With water and oil
flowing in your river
you shall know no dryness

In the days when life is cut short
by the swiftness of time
you shall last long in the palm of the earth.

Like honey
your sweetness will bring you
a hive of goodness

Like salt
you shall bring taste to our pot
which many a fire has cooked bland

As the sun keeps the promise
of her rising with the morning
you shall keep time
with the call of destiny.

Omalicha

iv

I waited
to bear the message of the spirits

carrying
the sacrament of newness without filth

riding
a chariot on the wind and water

proud waves shove the rock
wearing her warm scales off
and hauling it to the face of the sea

. . . silence alone comes to the rescue

the wind sweeps the sand off her feet
leaving the shores nude and desolate
Iyanga tingling the sleeping volcano

. . . silence alone comes to the rescue

Now
Ijele has come to the dancehall of bravery
Let *atinga* scamper into her hole

Ọbịalije has come
Let life begin.

Omalicha

V

Sleep awakes before the dew falls
On the bald peak of the mountain

Set out my child before the whirlwind
Stirs blinding dust in her wake
Set out into the narrow road of the four market days
Where you'll trade in time and place

Set out before dark clouds
Gather in the eyes of the sun
For you shall pass through paths
Running in roses and thistles
On a thousand crooked bends

Set out with your basket of hope
To gather wealth scattered in the heart of the earth

Ọmọ mi t'ó nlọ s'ọ́jà
Do not scatter the shrimp and gather its shell
Do not trade the seed to buy the leaves

Set out my child through fallow lands
And fetch abundance from the bed of the sea.

Omalicha

vi

They sought the divination of the seer
asking for the coming of a child once foretold
It was foretold of my coming
to fall in the season of cold and darkness

Onyemaechi
Onyemaụwa

I know the seedling growing
       in the womb of days
    yet to be born

echi dị ime

but *ogboo* told me that
       I am the mystery born of
   the spirits
unfolding on each waking pulse of time

mụbụwa
a lone child of twin destinies
       who has wrestled with demons
in hollow valleys and thorny dungeons

mụ bụ onye ma ụwa m
that is why I won't be lost
      in the bazaar
      of twinkling vanities
where men hawk
      the priceless wares of their souls

Omalicha

Ọ mụ bụ onye ma ụwa m

. . . how then can tomorrow hide
           mysteries in her
   womb
              when I am the seed
                      already born

mgbe echi ga-asa anya
the straying multitude
          healed of their blindness
shall see the words of the sage
          written within their hearts
leading them to that place
where they ought to have begun.

Omalicha

Like a lump of clay
in the palm of a potter
mould me
to tease the eye of beauty.

Omalicha

We Dream a World

We ask not
     for a world
          of our own
We fight not
     for land to own
We dream to share with you
a world crackling with laughter

We are green grasses
     in a field of wrestling elephants
Trampled under the jackboots
of those called to save
Yet we dream
     of a world
of angels in a banquet
     of ethereal bliss
 as we carry a mighty hope
in our little hearts
for a future we are dying to live

A lonely world it will be
unless you share it with us.

Omalicha

I Am

I am not a beast of the field
I am not a curse to the land
I am balm to the ache of life
I wear tomorrow like a crown

I am not your robot
But a being born of love

I am not a weed
To be smashed under your feet

I am not a thorn
Growing wild in your garden

I am a rose in bloom
Whose brilliance breaks through
The ugly and the dark.

Omalicha

My Name is Child

What is the name
The divine Sent of the gods?

Who is the knot of a nuptial tie
The lone spark of a holy bond?

Who is the thrilling melody
Under the deserted roof?

Who is the raindrop in draught
The pride that awaits hopelessness?

Who is the tower
The walking stick of an ageing generation?

I am the fortune hunting penury
My name is Child.

Omalicha

Paradise Path

the river bank
Frolicking

Buttocks bared

Whistling tuneless melodies
that spurn the strings of a guitar

   Where is paradise?

It is not the vacuous dolls
      moping at the children
or the children peering
      through the holes
      drilled on the wall
         with their eyes

Where is paradise?

Paradise comes to watch us
as we learn the ride of life
on the ascending hills
bruising the knees
and yet standing tall

Omalicha

Paradise
    is
       living
           through
               the
                  passage
                    of time

under
    the
       wary
          guard
                 of those
who
   have
      walked
         the
         path of Paradise.

Omalicha

Open the Prison Gates

The sun clothes her smile
In garments of dark shades
Even the moon hides her face
Behind the still billowy clouds

They cry that the world in us
   Is a slave in chains

Open
The
Prison
Gates
   And let the caves see the sparks
   Born of freedom's broken chains

Open
The
Prison
Gates
   And let the children set out
   Before the fall of dusk
   The
        Earth
           Cannot
              Journey
With her children
When the child
      That is the world
        Is fettered in chains.

Omalicha

The African Child

Burnt

Not charred
But glazed
Through the blaze of a thousand infernos

Dying

Reincarnating
Dicing for a noble deal
Sworn to pass his name on

Beaten

Not defeated
But sojourns
Through the furnace of a million tornadoes

He shall no more see
The night fall at dawn
He shall not die

The African Child.

Omalicha

Omalicha

ii

Born on the lush vegetation
　　　of vast greenland
　with the world
　　in his sack
hanging
on his shoulders . . .

　Like the Masai
on a long journey

planting greatness
　beyond the seas
and conquering strange lands

　The African child . . .

The earth is sown
In the solitude of a mother's womb
There, even like a blacksmith
She whittles the tool to form and destroy.

Omalicha

When I Was Born

She was moaning
In a labour of sweet pain
As she got abash in blood
When I was born.

She called me *Omalicha*
The name of a beautiful soul
Chanted to bring forth the season of rain
When I was born.

Her fingers dug a path before me
Her words set my tongue loose
When I was born.

 She is my mother
 Who built me a world of dreams

And made me, me.

Omalicha

My Mother's Sweetness

Sprout for me *ụdala*
Ụdala sprout
My father's wife has left me
The burnt crust of her cooking pot

Ụdala sprout for me
I hunger to taste my mother's sweetness
When your lips kiss mine
Sucking your milk

Ụdala sprout
And weave your roots in the belly of the soil
To tingle my mother's long slumber
Spread your leaves *ụdala*
And build a shade for me in the sweltering sun
Like she spreads her wrapper to keep me warm

Ụdala sprout
My father's wife has sent me on an unending
    errand
When other children bask in their mother's cuddle

Ụdala sprout
Feed my hunger to the brim
And make the taste of my mother's sweetness
                    indelible in my mouth.

Omalicha

Nnenne m

When life called me forth
　　You took me to grow
In the warmness
Of your womb

　Passion and toil played
On the grounds of destiny

Cradle crawled
　Into the arms of dawn

You brought me forth

Praise on my lips
Soaked in ballads
　Hailing you
　　The ancient blacksmith
　　　Of the inner temple

Nnenne m

Omalicha

And the weight of years
Bows you *down*

I would *Be your guiding rod*

L e a d i n g

you
        again
To the
        doorway
        of life.

Omalicha

Without Shelter

When the west eats the sun
And spits through the rear of the firefly
They hasten to the square
Limping on bruised soles
And licking their oiled fingers
Into the world of the story-teller

There
To a chorus of *nzamiriza*
He tells them of the hen and her chicks
And of the kite in a strange land

They start their long journey
The Hen never lets the chicks walk behind her
As she stays hungry to feed them
And shields them when rain pours

Suddenly kite hovers unheard
The hen and the kite tangle in a fight
Peeping from their hiding places
The chicks watch their mother in flight
Borne by strong talons

They scatter
Without shelter and destination
Wailing as they disperse
Not for the mother hen
Who will never return
But for the danger

Omalicha

that awaits them without her

The
    children
          wail
Not
      knowing
Not
      wanting
To think of a world

    Without a mother.

Omalicha

Away with your diamonds!
Show me the path to follow
Give me your hand to hold. . .

Omalicha

Someone Stole Mine

Streets of scattered shells
Of bombs and grenades
Has my cradle been

Million miles unmeasured
Through dusty roads
Has my journey seen

With this heart
That is a battle of worms
I bear the heaviness of hope
Hope which hangs unto the desire
To see another day

free
free from the searing memory
Of long dreary nights
I walk farther away
From a world ablaze with hate
Into a place where childhood
will be lived again.

Omalicha

The Country of my Childhood

Each time I stare at the waves
rushing into the arms of the ocean
I see me running back
to the country of my childhood
where many lost children find shelter. . .

Country of colourful dreams
where the earth and the meteors mingle

Country of dolls and unseen playmates

Let me come to you
and re-build my sandy castle
washed away at your seashore

Now take me back
I ask you
to the country of my childhood
where I am king

Take me back
            oh waves
                        on your soaring crest

to my country of vast playground
with no walls and barbed fences

Omalicha

Take me back
          oh waves
for this man has traveled far
into strange worlds
and mingled
               with
               beasts
                    and
          unfamiliar beings

This man
          has
               swum
                    and
                         bathed
          in many dirty fens. . .

O country of sacred memories
Let your gates be flung open. . .

Omalicha

I Stand At Your Brook

I stand at your brook
waiting for a drop of water

All rivers are sucked up in the eyes of the cloud
and the heavens will take long to shed her tears

I stand here waiting at your brook

I'm damned to ask for a pail of water
to wash my tatters muddled in dust and mud
not even a thimbleful to cool my head
pounded by ache

Just a tiny drop to douse this choking dryness

I'm still here standing on my wobbling feet
at the foot of your fountain
my trembling palms cupped before my mouth
panting for just a little drop

You have locked your river's bed
and hurl the key into the depths of the swamp

How soon you unremember
Sole warden of many springs
that the maker of all rivers
will come asking for his ocean of water
when even you shall seek just a little drop.

Omalicha

Never Hear Me

You see me sit in
The blistering sun

You pass unseeing

You see me shiver
 In the cold

You stare unseeing

You meet me
On the way to nowhere

You stride undaunted

You don't want your time
 Spent wasted

Another day you pass
Your heart pricked hard
Your hand was damned
To drop the alms

But you never stop
To know if I have a name

You may never hear me
Say a word
Not when you are
Too far to listen.

Omalicha

Stay With Me

Wake me
To the chime
Of crickets calling us
To the radiance of a new day

Wrap me
In your heart's warm embrace
And make my fear
Bow her knees in shame

I ask only
To be nursed by the old arms
Of those who gave me birth

Stay with me
Through this fragile road
And spoil me
With the wand of love
Even as you teach me
The ways of good and evil.

Omalicha

You Blame Me

Anini the armed crook
Whose fingers
Have shown many to their graves
Has a mother.

Adaji the wily whore
Whose waist
Has known many dances on quaking beds
Has a father.

Adamu the scoundrel
Whose pelted stones in the market square
Have cracked many skulls
Has a brother.

Akume the huntsman
Whose dane gun
Has killed without a trace
Has a sister.

Jail the crook
Truss the whore
Curse the scoundrel
Hang the huntsman
And let our house be washed of its curse.

But tell the hangman
To keep his noose dangling
Till he finds a river flowing from a gutter.

Omalicha

Where Dreams Are Born

See
It is dark
But the hue of shadows
May not be hidden from blind eyes

See
It is morning
Only the seeing eyes
May see the colour of sunrise

Seeing eyes are blind
Blind eyes are seeing

Dreams are born in realms
Where touchable beams of light abound

It is dark
But the blind eyes
See the colour of sunrise

It is morning
But the seeing eyes
See the hue of shadows

It is chaos
Only the hearing ears
May hear the call to flee

Omalicha

Break

It is mayhem
Only the deaf ears may hear
The warning to leap over the valley of danger

Deaf ears hear
Hearing ears are deaf

Dreams spring in the tranquil silence
Where sounds whisper mysteries.

Omalicha

We're Knocking

At the crook of criss-crossing cross-roads
Our blistered feet
Grow weary from long-laden trek

Hope stops at your door
                        gazing
Come rescue us
Whose hunger
has scavenged dry farms and dung hills

Knock knock
We're knocking

With our beaten aluminum plates
Stained by the dregs of long digested remnants
Hidden in those crannies
Beyond the reach of our little fingers

Hunger stops at your door
                        yawning

Knock knock
We're knocking

Feed our famished mouth mama
For hunger has filled our belly to the brim

Knock knock
We're knocking

Omalicha

If the wood is not burning in the hearth
And the pot lies empty to cook
Then wet our burning thirst
With drops of your breast milk

Knock knock
We're knocking

Shield us in your arm from the harm of the street
And lull us to sleep therein
To forget our days
Swallowed by the gluttony of distance.

Omalicha

ii

Ka children

I pour myself
As a libation of abundance

Fill your cup
With all of my substance

Drink me

Take from me
All of your days
Eaten by the road

Live me

Take me whole
On this altar of untamed love

Ka children
Mother has come…

Omalicha

Come to me
stick close
Close enough you can
smell my breath
And see how little you know me.

Omalicha

Sweet Doll

Sweet doll
Sit by my side
Smile to me as I sing.

Sweet little doll
Lie on my bosom
Caress my hair as I whistle.

Oh cute dummy doll
Come hold me
In a long embrace
As we wait for mother
To bring life to our dull moment.

Omalicha

The Child and the Coo Coo bird

O sweet child
Why do you giraffe
Through the window crying all day long?

O Coocoo bird
Why do you stay over the fence
Singing all day long?

My mother went
To the stream to fill her pot
Just like your mother
My father went
To the forest to hunt for meat
Just like your father

But the dusk has come
With neither of them home

I now play the drum alone
Sing aloud for you and passers-bye

Here is the drum sweet child
Let the beat cure the throb of our waiting
And chase this lingering loneliness
As we forget them that may never return.

Omalicha

Growing Alone

My mother who is a tourist
Married a voyager
And gave birth to me a hermit.

Seconds hold us together
       In moments
We're drawn centuries apart.

When I whimper
She says her career will crumble
If she dares cuddle me.
When I frown
He says I'll starve
If he dares sit by me.

The maid nurses me
I find friendship with carved wood
growing with toys who become playmates.

Someday you'll hear them say
I break the silver spoon stuck in my mouth
You'll hear them ask me why
Am I not like the brilliance of the full-moon
In the darkest of nights?.

Omalicha

Artist in Red

I can draw you a picture
Of a restless people
Chasing after life

I can draw you jolly rockets
A frowning sky
And dismembered limbs

I can draw you a forlorn city
Of live corpses
Where famished vultures
            hover endlessly for bread

I can paint you the hue of TEARS

            the aisle
            of hollow faces

Omalicha

Artist in red

Draw the narrow way of heaven
        Escaping the chase of hell

Paint the brightening cloud
Breaking the heart of darkness

Draw us
Oh artist in red
Moving
with
your
master strokes
Rising from graves
And waking on freedom's bed
Where we shall see you

An architect in blue
Who builds mansions
Out of smashed bricks.

Omalicha

This scream
Breaking between running lines
Of pain and laughter
Shall haunt your heedless ears

Omalicha

In Our Time

Here

In our time
Before our eyes
The world's wealth
Is blowing up in dust

Poverty in our time.

In our time

The pasture our fathers' cattle grazed
Is become a battlefield
The roots and herbs lose their cure
And sickness strangles at every touch

Disease in our time.

In our time

Every household shelters
A nation of hopeless refugees
Every man fighting
As if there was never yesterday
And tomorrow shall not come

In our time

The children are men

Winning bread for the household
While the infidels feed fat
And lean towards the grave

Here

Before our eyes
This sullen time shall see its end
When the earth will yield her harvest
To quench our dryness

In our time.

Omalicha

Cry Children

Cry for peace . . .
For justice who died
In the belly of silence

Cry for the days
Of bounteous waste and want

Cry for eyes dried of flowing tears

Cry
To purge the world of her venom

Cry
That you fight not their wars
Lest you die their death

Cry children

For peace who is to come
            for tomorrow.

Omalicha

The Song of Freedom

From the jungles of Africa
To the slums of Asia
From the ghettos of America
To the backstreets of Europe
We gather
Tearing
        The barricades
         Down in faith

From the four ends
Children gather
        At the square of life

        Calling out to love
To knot a thousand broken ties

    shattered by distance and silence

Omalicha

For Life's Sake

Bad words
     spoken

Infested seed
     sown

Vain tongues
     slaying

Life
    receding

But let the words run
Through your tongue
Swift to teach
The forgotten verses
Of salvation song:
     To heal the land
    I purge my soul
Of simmering vengeance

I give them back the gun
And forget my frail hands
Tilling the soil for the harvest
Of another season of life.

Like a wild fire on dry grass

Let your song be:

Omalicha

To
  heal
      my
         wound
I
 remember
          us
With
     our
        hands
           locked
For life's sake
Walking
      to
        the
          East
Where
      paradise
         is
          in

the midst of the gulf

That separates us.

Lost in the Dark

Suddenly the lights are turned off.

The curtains part in two.

A shadow walks in.

The voice bids me not to fear
Even in the pervading darkness . . .

Like I was running from a legion of demons

My feeble body quivering in the arms
Of he whose face is lost in the dark . . .

Who are you?

The hands ripped my dress . . . cold hands . . .

Innocence burns out. . .like wax
in the palm of the sun . . .

My voice
lost in the unheard cry of my private pain
grows thinner as the sparks of light
find their way out of the dark
while in pieces the curtains torn
clothe me in nakedness.

Who are you whose face is lost in the dark?

Omalicha

For Us Who Pant

When I look in your face
I see streaks of rage
carving maps of terror
leading vengeance to the field

We are at war

When I look in your eyes
I see specks of red
forming clots of blood
leaving smelly stains on the pathway

We long for life

When I draw nigh you
as we spoil for a fight
I hear your heart play for me
jingles of memorable *blues*

We pant for love.

Forget the fury
Of the wind
And unfurl your tent. . .

Omalicha

If You Ask

If you ask
Where the moon went in the day
You would want to know
Why the stars stay away
From the sun.

 If you ask
Why the earth and the clouds never kissed
You would ache to know
Where time goes without looking back.

If you ask
Where life was before it began
You would want to know
Why death kills without dying.

If you know
The source of a spring
You would ask
How it met the ocean.

Child
        These riddles have tied
        The tongue to the roof
And questions scurry into holes
        To find lasting refuge.

We Came to Play

We came out to play
The stars did not come
We began to chant and clap
The praises of the crescent
That the moon would not shut her eyes
At us waiting below the sky

The wind came whistling by
Laughing at our waiting.

If we ask Ọgọọ
Why the night is strutting by
       in the dark
He'll say the moon and stars
Are gone to the spirit land
To bring us a fortune
       on *Eke* market day.

Now, we wait.

We know not many hidden ways
Lest we find you out
But you must come lighten this sky
Who has grown dark with loneliness.

Come listen to our songs
Woven in our web of tales
Telling of births and life
Of yesterdays that never return
Of yesterdays that cling to now
Of todays that lie half-lived without tomorrow

Omalicha

And
   of
      many
          nights
             of
                tomorrow
When like Ọgọọ
                      We'll
                 know
              the
           ways
          of
       the wind and rain
Telling our children
                     to
               clap
            and
          sing
While they wait for you to come to play.

Omalicha

Send a Word

When I was told
Of the ambience of our mud house
I return to the times
With knots of questions and vain longings

Now, we crave comfort and live in mansions
Hewn in bricks and fancy reed

Ambience is gone away
Leaving behind lonely souls
That know no laughter

Alụ agbaa afọ
Evil has become tradition
Fathers have gone the crooked path
Taking with greed the treasures of the land
Mothers wild with desire abandon the homestead.

Virtue is gone away
Leaving behind unbridled greed
That knows no content

Chukwu abiama
Send a word
To the silence of our homestead

They say the world
Has opened her eyes wide
And now that the new light has shone
On our dark old ways . . .

Omalicha

Afamefuna

Maidens in a blind chase
Lose
     track
         in
            the
               crowd
            of prostitutes
And warriors lose strength
Marching at the cripples' pace
                     Children
           not
        knowing
   where they go . . .

Chukwu abiama doo
Send a word
That our homestead may not wither.

Omalicha

The Mad Woman's Sayings

I saw Akukandu whom they call hero
ploughing and tilling our father's field
With hoes stolen from the kin's grove

I saw him carrying from the farmlands
A truckload of yam
To store in his barn
For seasons yet unknown

I saw a multitude of children
Standing by the dusty road
 Licking their dirty thumbs
 And chasing flies from their mouths

The dryness of the land
Became the overflowing wealth of *Ogbuefi*
Akukandu. . .

He bought river beds
And channeled the flow of the stream
Into his clay pot

Akukandu has gathered the plenty of the land
And left famine scattered abroad
He has gathered food for his children
Yet to come in seven generations

He would eat to the bursting of his belly
Watching the barn overflow
In abundant rottenness

When he throws the crumbs at us
They swear his love burns the land aglow

The praise singers say
Words should be moulded and glossed
Lest our hero's heart be vexed
But words on my tongue carry the fire of lightning
That is why they call me

Mad woman of the roadside market

If I spit on those who doze
While Akukandu plunders the fields. . .

If
I
Spit
On
His mother
Who did not suckle this child. . .
If
    I
        Spit
            On
                That woman
 Who never told Akukandu
That the land and her harvest were
                    Before he came
They would say it's the madness
Of the mad woman at the roadside market

But I would walk the circles of the land
        Gathering the crumbs
To fill our children.

                                    Omalicha

Children
When
you
become
men
Do
   not
      follow
         the
           ways
              of
      the people's hero
You will die well
        if
     you
   listen
to
  the
    words
      of
       this mad woman
    of the roadside market.

Time Has Gone

Time has gone
when children greet
reaching to the ground
now they
        wave their hands
            hi in the air
 if their baggy jeans are sewn
        with no pockets

time has gone
when children wait
at the feet of the elders
paying obeisance
    to the proverbs
    of grey-haired men
now they concoct idioms
turned on their head

they follow unseeing
on the heels of tramps
dancing *okoso*
with the names of strange idols
tattooed on their buttocks and nipples

Time has gone
when the staff
guides the straying sheep
    to the pasture
even the cows of nowadays
would sue the herdsman
at the sight of a cane

The weed
has tangled with the seedlings
New wine
ferments with drops of the old

and the children

tipsy with *ogogoro* in their head
    hallucinate about America
where heaven-bound *molue*
off-loads her passengers

Time has come
 when *Nkemjika* will say to *Nothingwood*
     jidekaiji
if the marriage will beget them bastard children. . .

Omalicha

I see the mountain dip its head
In the gathering clouds
And I know where my destination lies

The Brightest of Mornings

This is the brightest
Of all mornings
Here in my twining race to the peak
I yield to the romance of sunrise
To bring me ravishing treasures

This is the brightest
Of all days
Here in my quest to serve
I'll hold a hand
To pick a star from the glimmering cloud

When rain floods the pathway
I'll build a boat to ferry on
If the flood rocks the boat
I'll grip a floating straw
To sail ashore

This is the warmest
Of all dusks
Here I count my harvest
Of green and gray
As I wait to embrace another

Brightest of all mornings.

Omalicha

A Thought for My Teacher

i

There he stands
With eyes and lips ablaze
With the fire forging my brain
Into a pot of knowledge
My sail across the barriers
Of ignorance.

My teacher moves his chalk
Carving specks of my thoughts
Into a masterpiece

The hero of all seasons
My teacher is.

Never will his house
Go weary of numbers
He must not be found wanting

god among humans

My teacher.

Omalicha

ii

Alànà
show me the way
at the footpath of entwined crossroads

You hold the lamp

Alámò
my head is a supple lump of clay
in your magic hands

èmi omo ilé iwé
who still bathes her belly with pails of water
asks to be soaked in your wisdom

the count of numbers will fail us
in our search to reach the soul of life

Teacher wa
àwa máá lo s'ójà
awa ma de'le

it is your word planted in our fertile souls
that will lead us through still and turbulent seas
of distant journeys

Teacher mi
rekindle the lamp
even in this age of sinking wisdom. . .

reawaken the flame
that we may know beyond the count of numbers.

Omalicha

Walking Down the Alley

The day is walking down the alley
Beasts are trudging home to rest
Men hang their hoes from their toil
While the sun stands glowing faint
Bidding us well with her rays.

Behold the winding of dusk
Like yolk glued to the heart of a shy sky
It is the colour of sweetness
Spattered on the canvass of our hearts
To keep our faces aglow
Even as the days grow pale.

It is the fulfilled promise of He
Who made love to barren Earth
Telling me my days are long
With a basketfull of seed
To be a planter sowing and thriving
Or a sluggard lagging and dying
When the land is yet unploughed.

Omalicha

There I Belong

In the depths of the clouds
Where only eagles soar
In the forest of mighty trees
Where only Iroko stands

There I belong

In the brooks of the jungle
Where only lions brood
In the east
Where life begins her course

There I belong

I'll dip my head beyond the cloud
like the soaring bird dares the wind
I'll dip my head beyond the cloud
like the archer's arrow on a flight to strike

I'll follow after
The flight of the Eagle
As it perches on the height of the *Iroko*
And watches the arrival of life . . .

Omalicha

I Bring You Peace

Peace of the ebony night
Mating with the sleeping sun
I bring to you

To wandering souls
And restless spirits

Peace of the bird
On the flight of the wind
I bring to you

To the broken cord
Of our sagging love

Peace of the needle
On the mouth of torn clothes

Peace of the incense
On a burning charcoal

Peace of the stinging bees
In honeycomb

Peace of the fish
And the flowing stream

Omalicha

I bring you

Stir
    peace
        that's
           asleep
Within us, brother
             To
      clothe
    us
    like a mother's warmth.

Omalicha

If I take you
From the source of rainfall
Through the depth of drought
You'll come forth whole

Omalicha

I Am Running

I am *running*
away
from the haunting past
Long gone by
By and by it resurrects
Raising dust and dipping its crooked fingers
Unwashed from yesterday's mess
Into my squinting eyes
Looking at the **dazzling** rays
of tomorrow's promise

I am *running*
running

running

out of ant-holes
Into boundless meadows

Yet *running*

With
        Shadows
  Fastened
            To my heels

Omalicha

Now I say to this past

My back is stuck
Against the wall
A n d t h e   wall
Against my back

And I call tomorrow to come

I am r u n n i n g

        A race
          On the track
Of days yet unknown

r u n n i n g

      a race on the track
      of days yet unspent

Valiant
Unbowed.

Omalicha

Untie the strings

Be
  The tree
  that lost her seed
 To the hurricane
See
    The grass
    Growing
 By the foot path
Become
     The sun
    Standing proud
    On the
          eastside

Me
   The star
   Who never
   Envies the day
You
     Fire burning in the kiln
  Me
   Candle glowing in the Temple
You
     lightning striking
Me
   Rainbow shining
You
    The
         Warrior
Who has won
  Many wars

Omalicha

Let me
Be me
With
    my
        words
   fighting my battle.

Omalicha

Clap

Clap your thumb
Clap my thumb?
Ridiculous!

Clap your forefinger
Clap my forefinger?
Impossible!

Clap your middle finger
Clap my middle finger
Crazy!

Clap your two hands
Better!
What a thunderous sound.

Omalicha

Now That She Calls

For Aisha Yahaya and Aisha Bima, poets in the bud,
and to all children who are called by the pen

If you are frigid
To the romance of the pen
The
Ink will spill

And stain the earth
With her tears

Caress her now
That she lures your fingers
And let the world
Hear her voice
On the pages of your thought.

Omalicha

He That Waits

He that waits for Mummy
To brush his teeth
Carries a stench when she goes away.

He that waits for Daddy
To dry his socks
Is barefooted on a rainy day.

He that always feeds
From Mummy's palm
Is without food in his plate.

He that waits for the housemaid
To clean his underpants
Stands ashamed in the square.

He that fears thorns
Has his farm
Overgrown with weed.

He that needs the whip
To set him right
Wanders a stray sheep.

He that waits for another
Will grow to have no one
Wait on him.

Omalicha

Talk don talk back to talk
so tey talk no get sense

Omalicha

Eye wey see

Eye wey see
And mouth wey no wan talk
Be like yansh
wey no wan sidon for house

Eye wey dey see
And mouth wey dey talk lie
Be like leg
wey dey waka kurukere waka.

Tongue wey dey hide for belle
go smell like hand
wey carry shit.

Make the eye wey see
Tell mouth make e talk
So that the hand
wey dip inside rotten shit
no go meet yansh for house.

Omalicha

So So Talk

i

Wey my broda
Who talk say e like me

Where you dey?

No be you dey inside mansion
How we go take meet under bridge
I for say
Make I shake you for across
But your hand dey too short
I no go fit reach am

You for say
Make you embrace me
But your coat too fine
My bodi go shame

Na for your talk
Na for only your talk
I dey hear say
Na you like me pass.

Omalicha

ii

Woman get belle
Man born pikin

Make we talk

Belle catch woman
Pikin born man

We dey talk

Man wey no see chop
Carry woman wey chop belleful

We don dey talk

Woman wey chop bellefull
don born pikin for bush

I say na talk we dey

Man wey go find chop
don follow waka loss

Na im we dey talk

Woman wey dey wait
don find man wey go find chop go

Na the talk we dey so

Man and woman go
Pikin dey for bush
Bush don catch fire go

Na the talk we still dey talk…

Omalicha

Wetin I Dey Talk?

Dem say
    water don finish
      for Bar Beach
I go cry
    make you drink
the tears wey dey my eyes

Oil is dried in the belly of *Oloibiri*

You go take fuel chop yam
Wey never grow for farm

Eko bridge is falling down

Our children dey cry

London bridge don fall
Our children dey call

Where you wan run go?

 I say water don finish for river
You dey piss for gutter

Come o. . .
Wetin I dey talk sef?

Omalicha

Look me for face

Na you look me for face
Call me bastard
Na you no ask wia my mama dey
Abi you tink say na from wood I come?

Na you look me for face
Call me *alaye*
You no ask as I take commot for road.
Abi you tink say I leave food
Wey dey plate come chop for doti?

Na you look me for face
Call me tief
No be my hand you catch for pocket?

Look me well
Na you born this bastard.

Omalicha

No Let Am Die

No let my enemy die
 Only let am die
   when life don teach am say
     goro no sweet for mouth
       as im music dey sound for ear

 Baba
   no let my enemy blind
     if you let am blind
      e no go see
       when I go waka comot for street

No let am deaf
   if you let am deaf
     e no go hear dis laugh
       wey dey scatter teet for my belle

 Baba
   no let my enemy die
     if you let am die
       who go follow me live.

Omalicha

ọbụghi akụ n'ụba
ọbụghị ọlaọcha na ọlaedo
sọsọ ịhụnanya gị
ga eme ndụ m osoo ogologo

Omalicha

Chere m

ụzọ dị anya
　　　　　ka ogologo agwọ
dị omimi
　　　　　ka aka gbara asaa

chere m

chere m
ebe anyanwụ awaghị n'ụtụtụ
mgbe kpakpando kpapụrụ ọriri

chere m

chere m
n'ọdịda anyanwụ
ebe ọchịchị n'achụ ndo

oke ọchịchọ a chụrụla ụbịam
　　　　　pụọ mbara asaa
 ikwu agbaghapụla ibe
ama nna tọgbọrọ chakom

chere m
n'ọdịda anyanwụ
ka izi m ụzọ m ga eso

Omalicha

Akwa Arịrị m

ọbụrụ na nne m nọ ya
ụwa m agaghị adị otu a
ọbụrụ na nna m nọ nso
ụwa agaghị akpọ m ihu ọjọọ
ọbụrụ na m nwere nwanne
akwa arịrị m agaghị echi gị ntị

ọbụrụ na nne nọ
aja m tara ga-eju m afọ
mana ebe nna m anọghị ya
mmiri m ñụrụ gbara m ilu
ụwa m adaala ngwụrọ
n'ihi na m gba aka nwanne

Ị ga eme m dịka nne
siri eme nwa ya
Ị ga abụrụ m nna
n'eleghị anya n'azụ

ọ bụrụ na m kpọ gị nwanne

Ị ga aza m.

Omalicha

ii

Nwanne dị n'mba
Nna dị mkpa
Nne dị ụkọ
mana m ga abụ
aka ga ehichapụ anya mmiri gị.

Ọnụ gi agaghị ata aja
Akwa mmiri gị agaghị agbagide
Kpọ m mgbe ọbula
Aga m aza gị.

Omalicha

Kpam Kpam

Kpam kpam
ka m n'akụ n'ụzọ obi gị

oku m n'akpọ gị
bụ oku ọkukọ n'akpọ ụtụtụ
oku ịfụnanya
ịfụnanya nne ji emeso nwa ya
nke nwanne ji emeso nwanne ya

   gbam gbam
ka m n'akụ n'ụzọ obi gị

   oku m n'akpọ
bụ oku ọfịa n'akpọ dinta
oku njikọta
njikọta nke egbe n'oke osisi

   ichikwana ntị
    n'ụda onu m
    n'ada ka ogene. . .

Omalicha

Nwa n'eku Nwa

Ọ ga aga ine n'ụtụtụ
Ọ ga akpa nkụ n'ehihie
Ọnọ n'ugbo mgbe anwu n'ada
Mana ọga azariri mgbe ọbụla akpọrọ ya.

Nwa n'eku nwa na eleta nwa
Mana ọhụghị onye ga akwọrọ ya
Mgbe ụkwụ jiri ya n'ije.

Nwa n'eku nwa n'esi ite
Mana ire ya amaghị ụtọ nri.

Ọ bụ onye ga eku nwa n'eku nwa
Onye ga agụgụ nwa n'eku nwa akwa nke ya.

Onye n'emegbu nwa n'eku nwa?
Onye n'emegbu nwa n'eku nwa
marakwa na awataghị ya n'nkụ.

Omalicha

Let not the dirge of the wailing minstrel
nibble at the rim your sleep
Glide home farther away from
they that cast their pearls into the grave
               Embrace
     little one
an eternity devoid of vanity

Omalicha

They Run Still

To the children who died in the Lagos bomb blast of 27th January 2002

The unguarded angels *run*
Holding hands
But slowly losing grip of life
In folds into the canal
They *RUN*
To find safety eternal.

The little lambs *run*
Ascatter from their shepherds
Tricked by the open arms
Of hyacinths
They embrace the canal
Pleading for free

The wounded angels *RUN*
Away from a city of bedlam
Through Hades
On their way to Heaven

Even as they *run* still
Never shall the black waters
Of the canal haunt their memory
For they are home now
Where their sleep
Shall know no labour.

Omalicha

In a Distant Reunion
To my brother Nnanna who has fallen asleep

i

A season of unbending strain
And a little grain
          Poured in a cup of pain
Half pierced underneath

Nothing became abundant

A thousand children
Groping to find their name
On the scroll of destiny

But
Faith fought the cold pang
Hitting with iron fist
On our fragile frame
Made frail by bouts of misery

In a distant reunion
We turn soldiers in many wars
And defiant captives of quiet battles

Now one stands
Over the astral bridge
Waiting for the conquerors' return

Omalicha

Who questions
His sleep at morn

Who asks
Who leaves the old till dusk. . .

ii

Your s i l e n c e

           Fills

                  The

Pages

                                     Of

           Our

                    Lives

Nnanna
sleep
soja man
ka chi foo. . .

                                Omalicha

Remembering

In memory of Loyola Jesuit College students who lost their lives to the Sosoliso Air crash of December 10th 2005 in Port Harcourt, Nigeria

i

From the shores of many worlds
Children gather
       In multitudes
on their heels to heed the call
There
The ripples of their laughter
rebound against the alluring sky
and rock the day to doze

Kpukpumkpuogene

Our play will go on
For we play not like men
Who build mounds over their eyes

Akpankolo

Our feet to the earth
      in graceful harmony
Will marry the drum
      droning in ecstasy

Omalicha

ii

Keep an eye little ones
Over the blurring cloud
To
  trace
      the
         homepath
             before
                nightfall.

               Leave
             us
           to
         our
    play Mother
   To live our days
  Before the jackals
 gather for carcass

Omalicha

iii

Danger
            fled
                    the
        streets
                        and
                                squares
            Washed
    her
        rags
                        in
                the
                                        stream
Crossed many farms and forests
                                    Over
                thatched
                huts
                                    and giant trees
    SMASHING down

like a coconut pregnant with soured water
Drowning the children in a sea of bitterness.

Omalicha

iv

Nwabụwa
Nwabụwa...
Nwabụwa o!
Dusk is *Falling fast*

And Mother calls. . .

Omalicha

V

Why has the palmfrond
Lost her green in this season of rain?

Even the chattering parrot cannot tell.

Now
Where are they
Whose laughter trips the soul
Do you hear still
The rhythm of the patter
Of their puny feet

Have you seen them yet?

They whose song resonates
Like two rivers kissing.

Have you seen them?

My children of the Nile
Children of the Niger
Children of Zambezi
Children of my womb
Children of the earth

Omalicha

vi

I
  run
     to
       the
          village
          square
Silence

To the market place
              I run
Emptiness

To the woods I go
Quietness

I
  run
    again
     to the riverbanks
Stillness

Alụ eme mụo

Long long I sit here by the streamside
Hoping the gods will show them
A homeward path

Omalicha

vii

Ayé nlọ aye mbọ̀

Rummage the creeks *Ayolo*
And bring home the wandering children

When you find them
Tell how mother waits
To rock them again on her bosom
Dancing to the sweetness of their song.

Ayolo ana m

The warriors are gone into the sacred grove. . .

Omalicha

viii

Oh you shallow dug graves
scattered on earth's four walls
Crack up your belly and throw them out!

You graves of Ethiopia
Let them awake
Give them up

You arid plains of Sudan

They lie still
In the graves of Liberia

They rot in the tomb of Congo

In the sewers of Haiti

They choke with life
In the Wilds of Djibouti

Through the Golgotha of Rwanda
They sleep in pieces

Omalicha

ix

We beat the *Igede*
with nimble fingers
That the sound of life
lead you on
Beyond the dark caves
and boundless deep
To hail your return
When the women
shall burst forth in new births
And this eerie nightfall
Will
close
her
eyes
in
unawaking sleep.

Omalicha

ADEIFE
(To Adeife Akindeko who was assassinated alongside her kid brother by unknown gun men on 20th April 2003)

A child of love
  born of lights

is gone home

Mortals weep

Hush!
        No dirge; children
        No wailing; mother

The heroine struts home
to where great souls are reborn
for the salvation of the barbarian man

Ifé ti dé'lé
from her twilight journey...

Blow out your candles

Adeife has burst into gleaming galaxies
speckled on the dark raiment of the cloud.

Adeife. . .
        fire ignited

Omalicha

on
   crossing
       our
          covens
            to
               heaven's bosom

           Blow
         out
       your
  c
  a
  n
  d
  l
  e
  s
for our eyes now are illumined

Adeife
When our sleep shall be long
Ká dààrò. . .

Omalicha

Till The Last Day

When the pallbearers tire
The poet will bear the homage
On her pen's shoulders
Waking the deep moments

Of life's forgotten vibes.

When the mourners' dirge dies
The potter's fire will burn hot
Leaving the night lucent in her lingerie

With no shadows of pain.

When the world's memory is beaten
By the forgetfulness of time
The artist will brush dust
Off the canvas

Tracing the fading lines of our tears.

When the hypocrites slump to bed
The saints will come awake
Invoking the heroes' names
In endless verses of psalms

Till the last day of infinity.

Omalicha

Where does this way lead. . .
This road I see
walking far into the distance

Omalicha

Passing Through This Door

Through this bound
                door
I
  walk
        a
         w
          a
           y

            Leaving hunger
behind

seeking food to fill my plate
seeking food to feed my soul
I shan't fail to find
For I'm passing through

This
     narrow
     d o o r
     of hope

Omalicha

This Long Road

This
    long
        dreary road . . .

This slender hope . . .

Tried in long
        long waiting . . .

This long road

        In finding destination runs
           deeper

This faith like an iron in a Blazing furnace

        Burns . . .

Omalicha

They Say I'm Lost

They say I'm lost

on the s
        e
        v
        e
        n
     cross
        r
        o
        a
        d
        s
L
  e
    a
      d
        i
         n
          g
           to the m a r k
                   s   e
                   q   t
                   u a r e

but I hear mother tell me

I'm walking on my path

. . . so long
. . . so alone.

Omalicha

Many Many Roads

i

Many many roads
Leading to many many streets
Where many grasses grow
On many houses of no people
Many blind people
Walking on dusty roads of lonely streets
Leading to no destination . . .

ii

This road mother
Where does it lead?
This road mother where seeing men are blind
To the glow of eternal sparks
This road where shallow footprints are swept away
By the breath of the wind . . .

iii

Many many roads
Of many footholds
Where intertwining roads run into one another
Where destinies collide
Embracing and parting ways again

But you must child
On this many many roads of lonely streets
Walk to keep an eye on your own path . . .

Omalicha

Untitled

She gulps the dryness in my nipples

For with love so unearthly I feed her

If it must

Let her hunger kill me

Let her pain tear me with its daggers

But I'm fed

Knowing there's a tomorrow

Because of my child.

Omalicha

Who is That?

Who is laying mines
When the children
Are on their way to the farm?

Who is planting bombs
Making orphans
At every blast?

Who is firing guns
When children seek refuge
With their heads high?

Who is shooting arrows
Kissing their flesh
With a nimble tongue
To lick and to poison?

Who is spreading this affliction
Serving the children a dishfuls
Of life's sourness
While they slugger behind time
Staggering painfully by?

Rid the land of lethal mines
And leave them to walk their miles
That the days of childhood
May not last long in the solitude of the grave.

Omalicha

Come Home

Seize the guns from the children
And send them home to light the fire
While the falling darkness
Still lingers over the patched roof

Leave the infants to run playfully home
That they may still suckle
Their mothers' dripping breasts

Ungird the children of the gangling armour
And let them trek their way
While the giant grass
Has not grown past the knees

If you must save us
The war of a thousand years
Lay the toy soldier
off the mouldering battlefield

Amidst this cacophony of bullets
Steer the children home
        That they may still remember
        The lyrics of moonlight songs

Let the warfront lie desolate
And let the children come home.

Omalicha

Start This War Anew

Drawn battle lines
　　　Unsheathed swords

　　　Shallow cuts on the skin
Deep scars in the heart

See jungle beasts feigning to be men of valour

Suns sleep
Nights rise
Yesterday runs into tomorrow . . .

No victor
All vanquished

A million armouries
　　　Desecrated lives

. . . talking rehabilitation
Where carpenters make clothes
　　　　for naked bodies
Frozen in search of tenderness.

Omalicha

I Pray

Here again on my knees
Before your mighty presence
The weight of words fills my mouth
Yet I know not what to say

Our house is *Falling*

Father!
Our house is *falling*

Now build us a new home
A big home to shelter the homeless.

Mould a new soul for them
Who say they are men
Take away the whip in their hands
And pour your oil of peace
To calm the madness in their heads
That they may see the world
Through the eyes of a brother.

Our house is FALLING
Father, do not listen to this mournful chorus
Seeping into our filthy mouths.

Father oh father
Even in your angered silence
Leave us not alive and blind
That we may see the bliss
Of just one day of peace.

Omalicha

Me no wan know

i and ya make the hug
Why throw me stones
From the other side
Still I'm gon kiss ya
With my bruised lips
Coz I see ya in green
     Hold ya in blue
   Drench ya in gold
  And adore ya in red.

Me no wan know
      ya is black
En white
    is no bright to i
For we
     is brown
  at the last of breath
Then why
     play ya guitar
       in a huff
  Cold or resonant
I'm gon frisk tenderly
Coz i drench ya in gold
    Adore ya in red
Hold ya in blue
See ya in green
Through the hue
   Of Jah's divine eyes.

Omalicha

At the bend
Of every wild street
I wait to take you home.

Omalicha

Mama Theresa
dedicated to Mother Theresa of Calcutta

Calcutta in the gutter
Beneath our mansion
Calcutta
In the abyss of our hearts

Mama Theresa
You bought heaven from the cherubs
At the price of life
And placed it over our heads
To shame the shambles of Calcutta

Mama Theresa
Teach us to stoop
Like you stooped
To sweep clean the house of Calcutta

Calcutta on the street behind our home
Calcutta in the lonely runway of our souls

Heroine of the *untouchable* generation
Mama Theresa

If our puny legs
Find your shoes to wear
They would learn to run
Like you ran the race immortal
Seeking eternity
In the noble call of Calcutta.

Omalicha

This Is Our Home
dedicated to Child Life Line, Oregun, Lagos, Nigeria

This is our home
Where we find a shade
From the wildness of the street
This is our home
Where we are stripped of rags
And crowned comely kings

This is our home
Where love is the law
That measures our lives

Here
We share a mother
On whose shoulder
Our dreams are born anew

Now
We can watch
The romance of the sun and moon
Through our window

Now
We can cry
And feel the comfort of many a bosom

Now we can die
And be mourned
For no one is afraid
To see us handle the mantle.

Omalicha

I Think Of You

When I eat
I remember
your plate is empty

When it rains
I think of you
shuddering in the cold

Though I may not come
to you
My heart follows your feet
to every wild lane
searching for respite

In my plenty
I feel the pangs
that punch your bowels
And my laughter tells me
how much of me you crave to live

When again I come to you
Wear for me a sparkly smile
Telling the story of hope
In a triumph over this lurking despair.

Omalicha

I Give It to You

All the words of my pen
All the rhythm in my drum
All the dance on my feet
All the sweetness in my voice

I give to woo the child

My ink will write your tears
Into mounds of laughter
My song will explode your pain
Into bubbles of bliss
Beneath my jangling feet
Shall your ache die

Where your voice breaks
There
My melody shall blossom.

Omalicha

Tell a child
that the world is an ocean
of bursting bubbles and bliss
and she'll swim in its changing tide

Omalicha

Tell a Child
In commemoration of Children's Day, 27 May; Day of the African Child, 16 June; Day of the Rights of the Child, 20 November

I know you're there
I know your story
That's why you are
My daily prayer.

It is you who bear the grudge
It is you who nurse the wound
Free your mind now
Rock the pain to death.

There is an end to this slavery
There is hope for freedom
It is not an illusion
That Heaven shall come.

Your discomfort is my pain
Your pain my tears
Your tear my wound
Every of your struggle is my battle.

For your sake I fight
For your sake to win
Till I see your pain die
With the passing of the night.

You are the gold
Crying to be found
In the garbage
You must not perish.

Omalicha

They'll kill
They'll destroy
But there will be
No future without you.

Meet me in the middle
To share this embrace
Let it be for us
A memory of redemption.

Put your mountain
On my own shoulders
For many miles lay
Before you to walk.

If I see you a coin
In a heap of diamond
I would choose you
To be my priceless treasure.

Smile to me like the sun
Does to the night
Telling the dark that her dullness
Is but for a passing moment.

If you live from the mountain top
You would see the promise of life
Where blind men
See broken stripes of hope.

Let me teach you to laugh
At the hard trifles of life
When they show up
On your journey's way.

Omalicha

The wealth of gold and silver
Count for rust to compare
Having you as my child
Which count for gain immeasurable.

I set the eyes of the world
On you my child
To see you are the beat
That gives rhythm to my dancing feet.

I chant your praise
Among a thousand princes
For you are the head
That bears the promise of my name.

Be the smile
The laughter
The longing
The ecstasy on future's dainty face.

Unchain yourself
Come live with me
In this place
So wide and free.

My hand is stretched out
Always waiting to touch you
With a love
So soft and strong.

I am the friend
Who would walk
Farther a mile
To bring you a smile.

Omalicha

We must not perish
In our pain
Let's hold one another
And build a bridge with streaks of our faith.

Dear child! You are one in a thousand folds
Exotic in a mammoth crowd
Most charming among the meteors.
You are just you.

What you owe
The ugly past is nothing
To the future, living.
Let not the days pass you by in silence.

You can touch me if you stretch your hands
You can speak to me if you open your mouth
You can come to me if you unbind yourself.
Meet me midway as I come to you.

Many days a frown follows a sigh
But a simple smile
From your heart
Can heal another in despair.

Would you be my friend
If I ask of you?
Would you show me the way of love
If I ask of you?

Would you search for me
If I got lost in the dark?
Someone like me without a past
Looking for a beginning.

Omalicha

There's a new sunshine
The kind that shines with intense newness
Let men put away the hearts of evil
That children may find their groove in this radiance.

Tell the warriors to sheath their sword
Tell the gun men to cease their fire
Tell weapon dealers to quit their sales
Tell them that judgment with a thousand allies
Shall bring home to us, peace.

You cannot be bought
For you are beyond a prize
You are the child
Your name's the future.

The white cloud on the azure sky
The passion
Between day and night.
That is you.

I am looking out for you
Praying not to lose you
In the street race.
Look out for my face.

Do not wait
Till we all die
Before you come
To the table of peace.

Hate begets war
War courts sorrow
A lasting sorrow cripples the essence of life
Pass on this message of peace.

Omalicha

Do not desire to die
In the hands of gory times
Charge your will and dare to live
And build the house of your dream.

Find the panacea for hate
And give it they
Who do not tread
The path of love to find fulfillment.

If you pierce the eye
　　　　　Of the sun
The earth
Will go blind with darkness.

We are weary of the silence after the inferno
We are tired of the torture of hatred
We are afraid of the seed of war
Tired. Terrified. We need quietness.

Keep the pity
Do the walking
Let the children
Take a rest.

Do not be caught dozing
In the warmth of your bed
When the children
Scream at nightfall.

i and i
Is 2 people
But we is greater
Than 2 as 1.

Omalicha

We are snowflakes
We can be better off
An iceberg
Only in a bond.

We are like lone trees if we stand apart
Rooted and growing together
We make a forest shielding us
Against the wrath of harsh seasons.

My last wish
Is to see
The guns laid down
For the sake of children.

If you were the sun
Where would your rising be?
If you were the sun
On whose face would your radiance rest?

Ignite the fire
That burns within you
Not to set the world ablaze
But to keep it aglow.

Play us a new melody
To chase the tune of old songs
Keeping the arena dull
With old dancing feet.

Hold your lamp for us
Who follow behind you
To see the hollow way
And save us many falls.

Omalicha

Hold your lamp
And keep the wick burning
Even when you pass
The way of the wind.

Make us see the world
Through the purity of your eyes
Changing our ugliness
With your enchanting beauty.

It is our faith
Not our tears
That will ferry us
Through these rivers of horror.

You are my pride
In the market place
My dance in the village square
I spread you to the eyes of the world.

Mtana mi
With you awake
My long night rest
Is without the ache of nightmare.

I may not live to see another day
But as I go resting on the other side
Keep this sign with you
Our hands together, bunched like a broom.

Na me dey beg you
Make you no carry your load give me
When I never
Start to waka my own journey

Omalicha

I am a part of every life you spend alone
I am the hand that scoops your streaming tears
I am the hope that says you must drudge on
You're the story that will soon be born.

I crave to
Open my eyes
And see no disease
Stealing away a child's tale of joy.

Every passing tick
Is a funeral in our house
But I still find a rainbow
Over our falling roof.

Your sorrow puts you
Behind the bars you build
Unweave the webs
And find salvation.

Think about the horror
Brought upon the children
By one day of war which bears
A hundred years of chasing after peace.

What the home lost
The heart would find
What the weapons tore apart
Love would knit again.

Teach me to hold a pen
And write my name
My hands tremble in weakness
Learning the skills of a gun.

Omalicha

They say the cut
Is too deep to heal
And the hurt
Too bad to forgive.

Yet some say
Keeping it puts on life
A heavy burden
 I choose to forgive.

My brother
Let's enter the paradise
Within our hearts
To begin the labour of a new world.

Bring your hand close
To my heart
And hear how loud
It calls for calmness.

If you reach out
And touch my face
You would find a river of tears
You can cup in your palms.

Only when we tie
In an embrace would you feel
How much of your caress
My scar needs.

If you lure me to see
The hope in your eyes
I can sleep rest assured
That tomorrow will bring me good.

Omalicha

Let the evil of yesterday
Grow dim before your eyes
That you may behold
The advent of a new day.

A patriot is not he
Who kills and maims his brother
But he who loves the land
And seek her peace.

Say you're not afraid to live
Say you will age
Say you will die
When the world can sing your name.

Do you hear the gnashing
At every interlude?
Do you see the distance
Those tiny legs have walked?

They are the children
Who have seen the end at morn
They are the children
Who beg you to leave the gun.

I've tasted a little bliss
So hard I learn now
To live through life's pieces
Waiting for peace embrace.

The beam of the crescent
Is dull for the night
But you and I like the moon
Will overwhelm the night.

Omalicha

If I were the sun
I'd flood your heart with rays
If I were the sun
I'd rise and set in your heart.

Omalicha

I Will Rewrite The Future
to Save the Children

bold on the blackboard of life
engraved in glistening dots of diamond

I will write that children are born
on the morning when rain
comes to bathe the dryness of the wasteland

Children ageing through the fall of many twilights

I will write that the children born
are suckled by mothers
whose breasts are bursting with pure milk

Men dancing to the bounty of many conquests

I will write that *uhuru* has broken her shackles
where survival lies in the passing of a needle's eye

Women waiting to be wooed in the romance
of the new moon

I will write that the warlord has burnt his weapons
where hate bows in repentance to love

Infants sleep in their cot without waking
to the *boom boom* of bombs
Children walking to school without fear
raging on their foreheads

You made war on the household
        of penury and pain
You chased poverty far
            into the solitude
    of the evil forest
You died the many death of the flesh
        to raise the children
from monstrous graves of despair

Bold on the blackboard of life
engraved in glistening dots of diamond

the earth will remember that
    you saved the children
from the flaming fire of hell
and brought them to the bosom of paradise
where nightmare melts into budding dreams.

I keep an endless faith
Walking these creeks
Paved with marble.

At The Door of Morn

I was
s
t
a
n
d
i
n
g
  at
  the door
                 When
          the
      night
    came
haunting
Wearing a hood
over a dark face

Windstorm slapped
the
walls
down

The roof caved
      into
   the ground

Dust and debris meddled
When the night came haunting

I saw blindness

Faith gripped my lingering fear
Light twinkled in my pervading darkness
And my giant stirred within...

I am
s
t
a
n
d
i
n
g
at
the door of morn

C
A S
T
I
N G

my seed for another earth.

Omalicha

Let This House Fall
To Sudan and her children

The house of Dinka
Was the house of Bari
The kith of Azande
Were the kins of Acholi
The trouble that troubled Bor
Was the agony of his brother
Until the evil days came.

The evil days
                    brought
                its
            rocking
        chair
    to
the house   swinging

        to
            the
                grumpy
            rhythm
    Of our silent pain

Many nights I pray
            Praying
        the
            prayer
        of
a lonely widow

Omalicha

Who is broken **IN PIECES**

  invoking the
               dying spirit
               of our love

I see the house of Dinka
          fetching water
     from
      the
      pot
       of
      Bor
I see the kin of Azande
          breaking kolanut
    in
      the
          palm
               of
               Bari

It is the dream of a child
It is the saying of the old
It is the hunger of time
That
     We
          Shall
               Wake
to find no more

The house of *Mugunga*
Where the sword
dangles still over our heads

                              Omalicha

I pray
  and
        pray
      in faith
Holding onto
            the
              tiniest
            streak
                of hope
    to douse the urge
          of vengeance

Let
    the
        house
          of
            Kibumba fall
                        to
              rumble

    that no trace
              of
          hate
        be
    found
      in
      its
    debris

wind wind
        BLOW
Dry wind of the Sahara

Omalicha

BLOW to tear the iron roofs
           on the
               house
      of
         Kitali

RAIN RAIN
         fall
Thick PELTS of the savannah
      fall to wash our stench
Pulling
       the
          flies to our sore

Build this home
Build this home
You who are clothed
            by
            the
    Nuba Mountains

Lo!
I have set my eyes on the new land of Sudan
The land of the rainbow
                people of the earth
The
    land
of children
         born and bound
              by
         Mother Nile.

Omalicha

Remember Tomorrow
To Rwanda and her children

Rwanda
   Call your children
Raise your voice
  Call *Sebahive*
From her hiding place
The dark cloud
    Is passing
     Over the palm tree
Kigali
Appease your warriors
  Hail *Sentwali*
    Fighting the ghost
 In his dungeon
Morena will rise
       In the midst
 Of pot-bound children
Rwanda
   Re-tell history
Call the scribes
To come scribble your testimony
  Telling of bravery and triumph
Remember tomorrow
    Rwanda
Remember the children
Born of new blood
undefile their souls
    Rwanda
You have died
Baptized in fire and blood
Risen
Rwanda
Live.

Omalicha

It Is Home

It's in the craft
  of the Spider
          spinning
          its web
It's in the art
    of the Beaver
            weaving
            its nest

It is home

It is tenderness
    found in a
      million
      measure
in a mother's hug

It is sparks
of laughter
    shared
in the fullness
of a father's embrace

It is home

It's
    in
      the
        comfort
              of
                a troubled head

Omalicha

rested
on
the
shoulder
of
a
friend

It's in the hunger of the soul fed
with the bliss of a brother's kiss

It is home

A faraway land
where
two
strangers
find love
A narrow bush path
where
two
foot prints meet

is called home.

Omalicha

Pool of Still Water

Pool
Pool of still waters
Still waters of dirt and dead flesh
Which has flown ashore at our doorstep

The pool runs deep
 Stinking
      Sinking
      Exhaling foul breath
We carry this pool in our hearts
Mucky pool of stagnant waters…

Come brother
Let love pull us
From the depths of this slimy pool
Wherein we sink and pass on

Come brother
Let's dig trenches
To let out this poisoned water

Life must not die.

Omalicha

Morning Shall Come

Many seasons of the full moon are gone
They in turn passed us on their way down

Many a nightfall closed in on us
trudging on our own long journey

wind
          came
                    spitting
                              dust
                                        in
                                             our
                                                  faces
daring us to trap her in our palm
for the rage we feel
Our stream emptied
                    herself
                              into
                                        the dells
and dared us to fetch her water
in the hollow of our hands

When
        the
              night
                        stretched
                                    on her mat
She found us waiting. . .

Omalicha

When
      the
          stars' twinkle
               twinkled out
We were waiting. . .

. . . beyond fear and death
we have trekked the belly of darkness
          yet we see beams
not of heaven's brilliance
        but the sparks in our souls
burning with the knowing
that morning's eye has not seen blindness. . .

Many seasons of full moon are gone. . .

They in turn pass us on their way down. . .

Morning has set out at the fall of dusk

Wait.

I see tomorrow with the eyes of a prophet

I see that

. . . morning has come

Omalicha

I Sing

Like a seer frenzied
With the unspoken words of spirits
Invoked by the substance of your love
I sing of you in the silvery run of the Nile

Like a maiden soaked
In the longing of her lover
Immersed in the flow of your musings
I sing of purity ripened
In the core of your womanhood

Strange suitors and distant lovers
Swim through seven rivers to kiss your feet
Monks and unfaithful husbands
abandon their call to worship at your altar

Perfection made whole

Nwanyimakalia

Hear *udu n'ogene* calling *ekwe n'ichaka*
To clap to the resonant whisper of the flute

Splendor *infinito*

Obìnrin bí ọkùnrin mẹ́ta

Listen to *Ayàn* with her nimble fingers
Calling out to the timbre of the talking drum

Omalicha

We are singing to the eternal charm of a woman
Who wears the risen sun on her face
We are singing to the ageless beauty of an Amazon
Who nurses patriots on her limber loins

Like a praise singer betrothed to the king's court
I sing of you

A love song calling for a medley of our souls
A song of love playing to the melody of our lives

A song I sang in the slave ship
A song I sang in the cotton field . . .

At your hallowed sanctuary
Words elude the chattering minstrel
Yet scattered in a thousand resounding symphonies
I sing of you in the silvery run of the Niger

Like a maiden soaked in the substance of her lover

I embrace you

Africa.

Omalicha

On The Two Sides of The River

People going
                People coming
Men living lives
        looking one on another
Through a film darkly
                    Men leaving
Women returning
Children building sand castles
Looking one on another
through the eyes of distance
Never meeting
Never touching
Waving our arms silently
from the two sides of the river

When we stand
bunched up on the bridge
kneading the widening divide
Our rainbow colour strikes
                    against
the silky face of the river
marrying our private lives

on the two sides of this long river

We die strange lovers
until we come on this bridge
to live
soul mating . . .

Omalicha

Acknowledgments

In different ways you spurred me to live this dream in the ways of your laughter, your pain, your dreams and your noble mission.

My Princess, Chinenye Okechukwu: our beautiful treasure where our heart is.

Chydera Daniels: for a thousand years of joy in those moments we shared when you came. Come home.

Fikuyin and Tumife Adebola: follow your own path little ones with grace.

I.K and Ebube Ojielo: you have come to fulfill destiny.

Tochukwu and Chi-Chi Nikita Akpa: you have brought the sun with you to lighten our world.

Aisha Sharu whose shining lights I see fire my zeal.

My granny Ujo Watuwogbodo Weneani who gave me my first wonderful memories. Mama *ka odili gi mma*.

Marion Sikuade: it is a haven you're building for them, an eternal treasure for yourself.

Michael Jackson: many children of the world have found in you a hero; their own hero. They've come to know the meaning of life lived in love through the gift of your passion.

Omalicha

My Hero Nelson Madiba Mandela, the fire you light in their fragile hearts shall burn to keep the earth aglow, even in moments of darkness.

Graca Machel: Mother, the children lean on your strength.

With the greatest sense of respect and gratitude to Unicef, Save the Children, Red Cross & Red Crescent Society for being a strong tower to the world's children and to You who has found a mission in the distress of the child.

Omalicha

Glossary

Pg 11　The sun has risen.

Pg 14　God of creation.

Pg 15　A beauty chalk of the Igbo descent used on special occasion to beautify a woman. No English equivalent.

pg 16　Welcome my child.

　　b.　Honey soaked in wealth.

　　c.　My child of gold.

　　d.　Welcome.

pg 18　Iyanga

　　b.　A royal masquerade in the igbo culture who comes out only on special festivals. It is the biggest and noblest in contrast to *atinga*, which is small and seen quite often.

　　c　The one who has come on a journey.

Pg 19　My child who's on a journey to the market.

Pg 20　Who knows tomorrow.

　　b.　Who knows the world.

　　c.　Tomorrow is pregnant with the unknown.

　　d.　The name of the Poet's grandmother.

　　e.　I am the world.

　　f.　I am the one who knows my world.

　　g.　When tomorrow shall open its eyes in sleep.

Pg 35　The Beautiful One.

Pg 36　An apple-like fruit that grows in the tropics.

Pg 37　My mother.

Pg 39　A moonlight chorus.

Pg 50　An onomaetopic sound produced when a blast occurs.

Pg 51　Ditto

Pg 54　An Nkanu dialect of Igbo origin that means 'take heart'.

Pg 76　The poet's great grandfather's name.

　　b.　The fourth market day of the Igbo people.

Pg 78　Evil has become tradition.

Omalicha

    b.   God of mercy.

Pg 79   May my name not be wiped out.

    b.   God of mercy we plead.

Pg 83   Igbo name for a fierce dance likened to the western disco dance.

Pg 84   An alcoholic dry gin.

    b.   A long yellow popular 'merry-go-round' bus found in Lagos, Nigeria.

    c.   An Igbo name that suggests that 'the one I have is greater'.

    d.   Suggests holding fast to the one you have.

Pg 89   The one who shows the way.

    b.   The one who moulds (a potter).

    c.   I, the school child.

    d.   Our teacher.

    e.   We'll go to the market.

    f.   We'll return home.

    g.   My teacher.

Pg 110 A place in Bayelsa, Nigeria where oil was first discovered.

Pg 111 A street urchin.

Pg 112 Hausa name for specie of bitter kola that grows in the tropics.

Pg 125 Let the day break.

Pg 126 Chorus of a moonlight song.

    b.   Ditto.

Pg 129 An Igbo name which means 'the child is the world'.

Pg 131 Evil has befallen me.

Pg 132 Life goes, life comes.

    b.   An imaginary moonlight tale character who comes to play with children.

    c.   *Ayolo*, am leaving.

Pg 134 A special kind of drum used by the Nkanu people of Igbo descent. Only Titled men dance its music.

Pg 135 Ife has come home.

Pg 136 let morning come.

Pg 178- The three most famous refugee camps in Sudan.
180

Omalicha

Pg 181 A Rwandan name that means 'bearer of good fortune'.
  b.   A Rwandan name that means 'the one who is courageous and brave'.
  c.   A messiah.
Pg 187 Woman, so beautiful.
  b.   musical instruments of African descent.
  c.   Where splendor ends
  d.   Brave woman
  e.   The drummer.

Omalicha